MONTICELLO

MONTICELLO

DILLON PRESS
New York

Maxwell Macmillan Canada
Toronto

Maxwell Macmillan International
New York Oxford Singapore Sydney

By Catherine Reef

Photographic Acknowledgments

Photographs have been reproduced through the courtesy of Monticello, Thomas Jefferson Memorial Foundation, Inc.; National Portrait Gallery; Pat Pugh, Division of Biomedical Communications, University of Virginia; Kendrick Photography (p. 22, 63, title page); Laura Pretorius, Division of Biomedical Communications, University of Virginia; Manuscripts Print Collection, Special Collections Department, University of Virginia Library; Tracy W. McGregor Library, University of Virginia Library; Holsinger Studio Collection, University of Virginia Library. Cover photographs courtesy of Monticello, Thomas Jefferson Memorial Foundation, Inc.

Library of Congress Cataloging-in-Publication Data

Reef, Catherine.
  Monticello / Catherine Reef.
    p.   cm. — (Places in American history)
  Includes bibliographical references and index.
  Summary: This is a history of Monticello, the Virginia country estate, which Thomas Jefferson designed and built as his primary residence.
  ISBN 0-87518-472-3
  1. Monticello (Va.)—Juvenile literature.   2. Jefferson, Thomas, 1743–1826—Homes and haunts—Virginia—Juvenile literature.
  3. Jefferson, Thomas, 1743–1826—Homes and haunts—Virginia.
  [1. Monticello (Va.)   2. Jefferson, Thomas, 1743–1826—Homes and haunts.]   I. Title.   II. Series.
  E332.74.R44   1991
  973.4'6'092—dc20
  [B]   91-15850

Dillon Press
Macmillan Publishing Company
866 Third Avenue
New York, NY 10022

Maxwell Macmillan Canada, Inc.
1200 Eglinton Avenue East
Suite 200
Don Mills, Ontario M3C 3N1

Macmillan Publishing Company is part of the Maxwell Communication Group of Companies.

First edition
Printed in the United States of America
10   9   8   7   6   5   4   3   2   1

CONTENTS

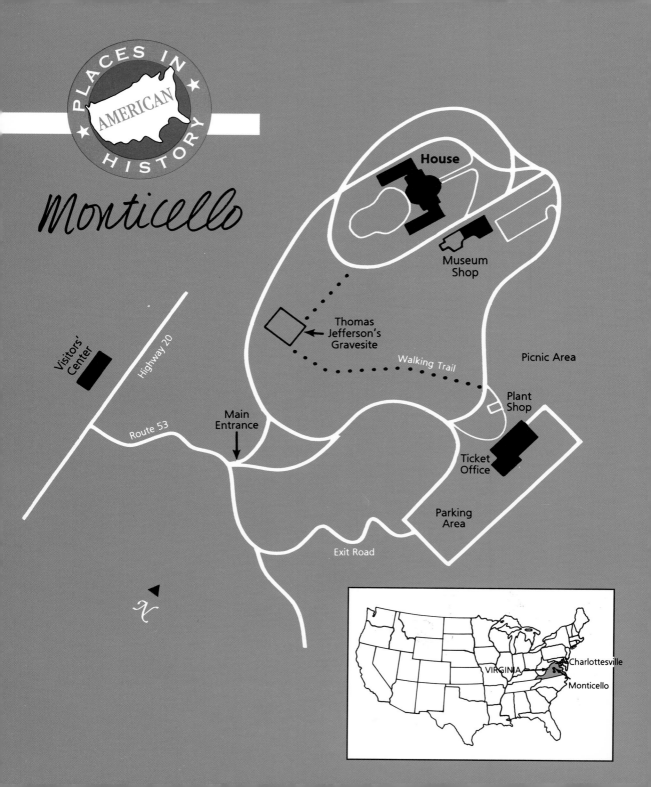

CHAPTER 1

THE HOUSE THAT THOMAS JEFFERSON BUILT

It was a warm summer day in 1753. Ten-year-old Thomas Jefferson, who lived in the English colony of Virginia, had gotten up very early. He and his father were going to explore the mountain on the family property today.

The two started the steep climb in midmorning. They cleared a path through the thick grasses and hiked through the tall trees growing up the rocky mountainside.

They finally reached the peak of the 876-foot (265.5-meter) mountain. Thomas gazed down at the ancient forests and lush Virginia farmland spread out below. To the west were the Blue Ridge Mountains. To Thomas, it seemed like all kinds of adventures awaited him in the vast, unexplored wilderness beyond the mountains.

This mountain would become the place Thomas loved best in the world. In time, he would design and help build his house on top of the mountain. That house, called Monticello, which means *little mountain* in Italian, would become one of the most famous mansions in the United States.

The trip to the top of the mountain was just one of the adventures that Peter Jefferson shared with his elder son. Thomas's father taught him how to hunt, make maps, and live in the wild.

The Jeffersons lived on an estate called Shadwell. Many travelers to Williamsburg, the capital of the Virginia colony, spent the night at Shadwell. The visitors included Outassate, the chief of the Cherokee nation. The chief gave Thomas a canoe paddle as a gift. Thomas developed a deep respect for Native Americans—and a longing to explore the West.

Then tragedy struck. Thomas Jefferson's father died suddenly. The fourteen-year-old boy had inherited the family estate—and the responsibilities that went along with it. There was a 5,000-acre (approximately 2,000-hectare) tobacco plantation to manage. His sisters and baby brother looked to him for guidance.

The best way to fulfill his responsibilities was to get an education, he decided. This is what his father would have wished. A family friend and guardian, John Harvie, agreed to look after the family and estate.

Thomas finished his studies and assumed management of the tobacco farm. But he had been to the top of the mountain and knew that there was a whole world beyond Shadwell. His dedication to human liberty and love for humanity would lead him into that world. And he would play a central part in shaping the development of the United States of America.

Jefferson wrote the Declaration of Indepen-

dence, the document that proclaimed America's freedom from England in 1776. Twenty-five years later, he became the third president of the United States. He excelled as a scientist and thinker. He also gained fame as an architect, a person who designs buildings.

Jefferson began the construction of Monticello, the thirty-five-room house that he designed, when he was twenty-six years old. At the same time, he became active in politics.

Thomas would not complete Monticello for forty years. The needs of the newly independent United States often called him away—to Philadelphia, Washington, D.C., and even France. Only after he retired was he able to truly settle in at Monticello. For the rest of his life, he dedicated himself to the pursuits he loved best—his daughter and grandchildren, his gardening, and the improvement of Monticello.

Monticello was Thomas's laboratory. Here he experimented in architecture. He adapted some

Thomas Jefferson, third president of the United States.

It took Thomas Jefferson more than forty years to complete Monticello to his satisfaction.

designs, such as a domed roof and tall, columned porches, from European architects. He connected his library, study, and bedroom to create a private "minihouse" within the house. He also turned his entrance hall into a museum.

Thomas wasn't afraid to change the way the house looked when he got a better idea. Just as a person changed and developed over time, so should his house, he thought. Thomas Jefferson the architect was always "putting up and pulling down."

Thomas Jefferson pursued other activities at Monticello, too. He grew hundreds of different vegetables and flowers, kept detailed records about the weather and his gardens, and collected books, paintings, and sculpture. He had many devices built that would serve the family, including a clock that tells both the time of the day and day of the week.

More than 160 years after Thomas Jefferson's death, Monticello still reflects his personality, interests, and ideas. It is no longer a private home, but a carefully restored historic site.

Entering the house is like going back in time to Thomas Jefferson's world. The furniture, dishes, musical instruments, and other objects Jefferson owned are set up to look as though he and his family still live there. Flowers and vegetables grow in orderly gardens that have been planted to look as they did when Thomas Jefferson was alive. It's easy to imagine fresh-picked vegetables cooking on a cast-iron kettle in the kitchen, which is one of the dependencies, or work areas.

Each year, over 500,000 people travel to Monticello, which is located in Albemarle County, in central Virginia. And Thomas Jefferson is still inspiring people. His architecture shows them that they, too, can design their own houses. His flower and vegetable gardens give people ideas about what to plant in their gardens. Everyone comes away knowing more about Thomas Jefferson—statesman, author, scientist, architect, and great American.

This is the story of Thomas Jefferson and the house that he built.

CHAPTER 2

A Home on Little Mountain

Thomas Jefferson's education opened up a whole new world for him. At the boarding school he attended, he read about faraway places and made some good friends. One, Dabney Carr, often came home with Tom on the weekends. The two boys rode horses up to "Tom's Mountain." They reined in their horses at an old oak tree on the mountainside. This became their secret hideaway.

One day, Thomas decided, he would build a house on the mountain near the old oak tree. But for now, he had to finish his studies.

In 1760, at the age of seventeen, Thomas entered the College of William and Mary in Williamsburg. With three hundred homes and a thousand people, Williamsburg was the biggest city he had ever seen. Thomas saw his first play there and attended horse races, concerts, and dances.

The students got to watch the Virginia House of Burgesses in session. As Thomas Jefferson listened to the lawmakers debate, he never imagined that he, too, would become a government leader.

Thomas Jefferson's studies were guided by Dr. William Small, one of his professors. Small was impressed by the young student's desire to learn and encouraged his interest in everything from political debates to forecasting the weather. Dr. Small introduced Thomas Jefferson to Gov. Francis Fauquier of Virginia and George Wythe, the famous lawyer.

At the governor's palace, Thomas met famous men from around the world. Their dicussions, about everything from new discoveries to the latest books to ancient works of art, often lasted late into the night. Thomas Jefferson started to consider things as a thinking man of the world, instead of a boy from a small town in Virginia Colony.

At nineteen, Thomas began studying law. His teacher, George Wythe, directed Thomas to write down his own interpretation of the ideas he read in law books. Thomas found that this helped focus and refine his own ideas, and he enjoyed this type of "debate." He used a special journal called his "Commonplace Book" for this purpose.

Thomas became a lawyer in 1767, the same year he decided to begin designing and building Monticello. There was no school for architects in Virginia, so he turned to books for help.

Thomas studied the sketches of the Italian architect Andrea Palladio, one of the most important architects in the sixteenth century. Palladio's buildings had wide open porches, called porticos, which were supported by tall stone columns. They had sleek, straight lines, and seemed to reach up to the sky.

They didn't look at all like the box-shaped structures with rows of small windows that Thomas had seen in Virginia. The colonies had inherited this style of architecture from England, and Thomas wanted something different.

Except for the window glass that would have to be imported from England, he decided to build the entire structure from native American materials. Nails and woodwork for the house would be made in the craftsmen's shops at Shadwell. The bricks would be made by mixing sand, Shadwell's reddish soil, and water together. A kiln for baking the bricks so they wouldn't crumble would be built on the mountain.

Thomas had decided to use brick instead of the wood most builders used because a wood-frame house could easily catch on fire.

After making hundreds of sketches, Thomas was satisfied with the design of Monticello. The house would be two stories, with tall columned porticos on each level. Two smaller cottages, called pavilions, would be built alongside the main house; L-shaped wooden walkways, or terraces, would connect these to the house. The kitchen, laundry, smokehouse, carriage house, and icehouse would be underneath the terraces, so they wouldn't block the mountain view.

Not many people built houses on top of mountains at that time. There were no wells on the property, so water would have to be carried in from a distance. There were no roads, and building them up the steep mountainside would take years. The site also had to be leveled so that when the foundation was laid, the house wouldn't be crooked.

Thomas didn't let these things stop him. Monticello was the place he loved best in the whole world, and that was where he wanted to live.

Two years after construction on the house

started, Thomas was elected to the Virginia House of Burgesses. Now he would be taking part in the government, instead of just watching others debate. Although Thomas was often away working as a lawmaker, lawyer, and farmer, the construction continued.

In 1770 workmen completed the first cottage, the South Pavilion. Thomas used the one-room structure as a laboratory. The South Pavilion survived all the design changes Thomas made over the years.

During one of Thomas's business trips, tragedy struck at Shadwell, the Jefferson family estate. The house, which was made of wood, burned to the ground. Thomas's family escaped harm, but his enormous book collection had been destroyed. At first he thought the only book that survived was one that he had lent to a friend. Luckily, his own journals—the "Commonplace Book," "Account Book," and "Garden Book"—were in his little cottage at Monticello.

Shadwell was rebuilt, but Thomas moved into the little cottage on the mountain. That fall, while working in the House of Burgesses, Thomas met and fell in love with the young widow Martha Wayles Skelton. Many other men also wished to marry cheerful, musical Martha. But when two suitors came to call on Martha, the sound of voices stopped them at the door. Inside, Tom and Martha were talking and laughing. The couple sounded so happy that the suitors left.

Thomas and Martha married on January 1, 1772. They began life together in Monticello's South Pavilion. They liked its cozy size, since they loved being together. Over the next ten years they would have six children, but only two daughters, Martha (called Patsy) and Maria, lived to be adults.

While Martha kept records of kitchen supplies and household needs, Thomas kept records of the gardens and orchards he planted. Thomas

The South Pavilion, or "Honeymoon Cottage."

Jefferson treated his vegetable and flower gardens and his fruit orchard as a huge experiment, and grew hundreds of varieties of plants. There were nineteen different kinds of fruit and nut trees, including apple, peach, pear, cherry, apricot, almond, and pecan. He planted twenty-two different varieties of his favorite food—the pea.

When the main house was almost ready,

Thomas bought furniture and cabinets from craftsmen in Williamsburg. He restored his library, which now contained over one thousand books. He built a "roundabout," the first of four roads circling Monticello.

In 1775 the Jeffersons moved into the main house. Life at Monticello was full of happiness, but outside its borders there was a lot of turmoil. The seeds of revolution against England were being sown in the thirteen English colonies.

Many people didn't think it was right to obey English laws, since the colonies had no representation in the British Parliament. They thought the colonies should unite to become a free, self-governing nation. They felt that paying money to England in the form of taxes was wrong, too, since the colonies received no benefits from doing so.

Thomas believed that people were born with certain rights—freedom being the basic one. Members of the House of Burgesses debated long hours about the issue of freedom from England.

At one meeting, Patrick Henry, the great orator, or speaker, declared, "I know not what course others may take, but as for me—give me liberty, or give me death!"

Tall, red-haired Thomas Jefferson was no orator. One listener remarked that when he stood up to speak, his voice "sank in his throat." He could express his ideas in writing very well, though. While Patrick Henry made speeches, Thomas wrote a paper about Americans' rights. The article, called "A Summary View of the Rights of British America," was read throughout the colonies, and even in England. To protect Thomas from harm or possible arrest by the English government, it was signed "By a Native and Member of the House of Burgesses."

The English began cracking down on pro-testors, but this only united the colonies further. In June 1776 representatives of the thirteen colonies held their second Continental Congress.

This time, they chose Thomas to write the Declaration of Independence. The Declaration of Independence, now one of the most famous documents in American history, stated that the colonies were free of English rule.

Thomas called upon all the books he had read, the ideas he had written in his "Commonplace Books," and his experience with the people themselves to write the document.

Day and night he sat at his specially made portable desk, working on the document. At the end of two weeks, Thomas had a draft which clearly outlined the principles upon which the new government would be based. The powerful document stated that "all men are created equal," and that they had certain rights that could not be taken away from them; those included "life, liberty, and the pursuit of happiness."

Benjamin Franklin, John Adams, and other Continental Congress members reviewed Thomas's text. They changed little, although the section that condemned slavery was taken out. Representatives of the Southern colonies would not support this, since the farmers in the South depended upon slave labor. Twelve of the thirteen colonies ratified, or accepted, the declaration on July 4, 1776.

The Revolutionary War followed swiftly on its heels. Thomas Jefferson's stirring words gave many the courage to fight against England. The Declaration of Independence gained fame throughout the world. It would later inspire France to draft its Declaration of the Rights of Man in 1789.

The battleground of the Revolutionary War included the new state of Virginia, where Thomas was governor. In 1781 the British "redcoats," named for their scarlet uniforms, seized Richmond, the new capital. A detachment of troops headed toward Monticello to arrest Governor Jefferson.

To ensure his family's safety, Thomas took them to a friend's house while the British searched for them at Monticello.

The war years were upsetting and difficult for Martha Jefferson, even though Thomas did everything he could to make her feel comfortable. After she gave birth to a baby girl in 1782, she became very weak. Thomas barely left her side during this time. He wrote to his friend James Monroe, "Mrs. Jefferson has added another daughter to our family. She has been ever since and continues very dangerously ill."

Four months later, at Monticello, Martha Jefferson died. The infant daughter lived only two years.

CHAPTER 3

A NEW MONTICELLO

Nothing seemed to ease Jefferson's grief after Martha died. He spent weeks pacing across his bedroom floor and taking long horseback rides on the mountain. "A single event wiped out all my plans and left me a blank which I had not the spirits to fill up," he told a friend.

What helped Thomas fill the hole in his life was his election to the Continental Congress in 1783. For the next six months, he assumed a leadership role in helping plan for new states in the West. He tried to outlaw slavery in those states but did not succeed. He proposed a new unit of money, the dollar, as the basic currency in the United States and suggested it be divided into one hundred parts, called cents.

Thomas also found time to write to his daughter Patsy, advising her on everything from what she should study to how she should dress!

On May 7, 1784, Thomas was asked to become a minister to Europe. The job was too important for him to pass up. His goal was to set up trade agreements with the Europeans. First he would have to convince them that America was not just a group of settlements in the woods. It was a strong and growing nation.

To prepare himself, Thomas toured the North to get a feeling for the people who lived in America's territories. On July 4, 1784, he and Patsy boarded the ship to Paris, where he would be based. Thomas also took along another family member—his parrot named Shadwell!

While overseas, Thomas became the minister to France. During the next four years, Thomas made friends for himself and the United States, and became known as an intelligent man who represented a free and prospering society.

In Europe, Thomas had the chance to see all the paintings, sculptures, and buildings that he had read about in books. He especially liked the design of the Maison Carrée, an ancient Roman temple in southern France that had a tall, columned portico. He sketched its design and sent it to Virginia. His drawing became the basis for the Virginia state capitol. He took careful notes as he watched work progress on the domed roof of the Hôtel de Salm in Paris.

Thomas could picture Monticello with a single columned portico like the Maison Carrée's and a dome like the Hôtel de Salm's.

Thomas Jefferson admired French parquet floors, made with small pieces of wood fit together like a puzzle, and designed one for Monticello's parlor. The French slept in "alcove beds," tucked cozily into walls, and he planned to do the same at Monticello. He also wanted to try some of the farming methods he had observed in Europe in his own gardens.

The Jeffersons returned home in 1789. Eighty-six crates filled with furniture, books, paintings, and gifts came with them! Thomas was eager to start reconstruction at Monticello, but another job awaited him. George Washington had just been elected president, and asked Thomas to be secretary of state. Thomas knew that the creation of a solid government was extremely important to America's future, so he put his plans for Monticello on hold and accepted the post.

In 1793 the enlargement and transformation of Monticello began. Workers tore down the two-story porch, which would be replaced with a single-story columned portico. They removed the slanted roof. They reconstruction would take sixteen years.

Thomas had to trust that the craftsmen and carpenters knew what they were doing, because for much of that time he was serving in the government. He was in Washington, D.C., the new capital, serving as vice president under John Adams, the second president. During this time he counted the days until he could return to Monticello.

In 1801 he became the third president of the United States. One of the most important things he did was arrange the purchase of the unexplored land between the Mississippi River and the Rocky Mountains from France. This was called the Louisiana Purchase, and it doubled the size of the United States. He sent two explorers, Meriwether Lewis and William Clark, on an expedition to map this frontier and make note of all they saw, from the grizzly bears to new kinds of plants to the fish in the rivers.

In 1809 Thomas Jefferson completed his second term as president. He piled his belongings in a coach and rode back to Monticello.

Although he was sixty-six years old, Thomas felt that his life was just beginning. He was now free to spend as much time as he wanted improving Monticello. He was able to oversee his farms and textile shops. Most of all, he was happy to be reunited with his only remaining daughter, Martha, and his grandchildren, who lived at his estate.

Monticello looked different from any other house already built in the United States. Thomas had designed it so that from the outside it looked like a tall, one-storied house. Inside, though, there were three stories. At the top of Monticello was the "Sky Room," an eight-sided room with a dome-shaped roof that had a large, circular window at the top. The dome was the first ever constructed on an American home. The parlor's parquet floor was the first in America, too.

Thomas did away with the grand staircases common to most large American homes and replaced them with narrow staircases tucked away in hallways. He added an entrance hall that served as a museum full of Native American

The entrance hall at Monticello, where Jefferson received his visitors.

artifacts and other natural-history specimens. Monticello also had an indoor bathroom, which was rare at that time.

Martha and her family slept on the third floor. Each bedroom contained an alcove bed. Thomas's private living quarters were on the first floor. They consisted of his library, study, and bedroom, which were connected. This was

The "Sky Room" at Monticello, an eight-sided room with a dome-shaped roof.

Each bedroom contained a cozy alcove bed.

his sanctuary, and no one entered without an invitation.

The library housed thousands of books, one of the most extensive private collections at that time. Thomas's measuring gadgets, telescope, and various devices he had constructed were kept in his rooms, too. His alcove bed fit into a passage between his bedroom and his study.

The view from Jefferson's bedroom into his study, where each morning he wrote letters with his polygraph and pursued his studies.

In the study, Thomas had a chair with candlesticks attached to it for light. His two desks were filled with paper, ink, and other writing supplies. One desk, the fold-up portable desk that he had written the Declaration of Independence upon, was in an unusual location, but one that made sense. It sat at chest-high level on a shelf, so Thomas could write while standing.

Besides improving his mind through reading and writing, Thomas became a master gardener. A greenhouse for his experiments with flowers and vegetables adjoined his rooms. He wrote in his "Garden Book" that though he was an old man, he was a young gardener.

There was a joinery on the estate, where furniture and ornamental woodwork for Monticello were made. The grounds included stables, where horses were groomed and fed. There was a blacksmith shop, where iron was forged into tools, carriage parts, and horseshoes.

Most of the day-to-day running of the farm was done by slaves. Many lived in a section of the estate called Mulberry Row. Two hundred African-Americans lived in slavery at Monticello. Thomas Jefferson had inherited this system of slavery, and during his lifetime, he was not able to change it. To his credit, he had tried to outlaw slavery in the Northwest Territory, but this bid had failed.

Isaac Jefferson, one of Thomas Jefferson's slaves.

The parlor, with its parquet floor, where the Jefferson family gathered for games, reading, and music.

Thomas and his family ate dinner around 4:00 P.M. each day. Vegetables from Thomas's garden made up most of the meal. His grandchildren loved spending the early evening hours in the parlor with him. And it was Thomas who taught them many games. They also told stories, played chess, and made music.

Thomas shared his house with his friends,

too. Some people stayed over for weeks. It wasn't unusual to have up to twenty people staying overnight. Thomas treated his guests well, serving elaborate meals.

It was around this time that the War of 1812 against the British broke out. In Washington, D.C., the British burned down the Capitol, which housed the congressional library. Thomas did what he could to help: He offered his 6,700-book library to Congress at whatever price they felt willing to pay. The government used those books to start the Library of Congress, and Thomas immediately began assembling another library!

Thomas would give this new book collection away—to the University of Virginia, Virginia's first public university. Thomas designed and supervised its construction, developed its course of study, and hired its professors. It was the first public university that allowed people of all religions to attend.

Thomas chose Charlottesville, which was near Monticello, as the site of the new university. Charlottesville was at the center of Virginia and easy for all residents to reach.

Although Thomas was seventy-five by this time, each morning he mounted his horse named Eagle and rode to the building site. The university's Rotunda reflects his interest in Roman architecture. It is a small copy of the Pantheon of ancient Rome, which is round and domed, with a tall, columned portico.

During the time the university was being built, something happened that would threaten the future of Monticello. Years earlier, Thomas had helped a friend get a $20,000 loan. When the friend could not repay the debt, Thomas became responsible for it.

Thomas could only afford to pay off some of the interest on the loan. This troubled him greatly, but he never said a word against his friend.

Thomas Jefferson frequently served elaborate meals to guests in the dining room.

© *Thomas Jefferson Memorial Foundation, Inc.; H. Conroy*

Thomas's financial problems grew, though, as the interest accumulated. He tried to sell some of Monticello's lands, but was unsuccessful. He worried that Monticello might have to be sold.

The Rotunda at the University of Virginia, a campus building that Thomas Jefferson designed.

CHAPTER 4

MONTICELLO FOR SALE

Although Thomas Jefferson had not slowed down after he retired from public office, age was catching up to him. In March of 1826 he became very ill. When he recovered, he was much weaker.

He still insisted on riding Eagle, but it was hard for him to hold on to the horse's reins. The gentle horse just patiently guided its master through the beautiful forest paths of Monticello.

A few months later, Thomas Jefferson received an invitation to celebrate the fiftieth anniversary of the Declaration of Independence. Thomas knew that the long carriage ride to Washington, D.C. would be too difficult for him.

On the day of the celebration, July 4, 1826,

Thomas Jefferson's family gathered at his bedside. The eighty-three-year-old man was seriously ill, and at 12:50 P.M. he died.

Thomas Jefferson was buried beneath the old oak tree on Monticello, next to his beloved Martha. The monument at his burial site listed three important accomplishments of his: author of the Declaration of Independence and the Statute of Virginia for Religious Freedom, and the founder of the University of Virginia. That was what he had wanted written on his gravestone.

Thomas Jefferson's family took over his debt. To raise money to pay it off, they sold Monticello to James Barclay in 1831.

Barclay turned the estate into a silk factory. He grew mulberries to feed his many silkworms. They were supposed to spin silk cocoons, which he hoped to transform into silk. His venture was more difficult than he expected, and he gave up after one year.

In 1834 Lt. Uriah P. Levy of the United

States Navy purchased Monticello. Thomas Jefferson was one of Levy's heroes, and he cherished the former president's home. Then Levy died, and Monticello stood vacant.

The care of the house fell to a farmer. In the grand flower gardens, he built pigpens. He used the parlor as a storeroom for bins of grain. He didn't fix the broken windows and fences. The house became run-down.

During the Civil War, which began in 1861, the house was taken over by the Confederate government. The Confederacy was made up of several Southern states that had left the Union, or Northern states, to form their own nation. One important reason for the war was that the Confederacy practiced slavery, which the Union wanted to abolish. Jefferson himself had stated years earlier that all human beings had the right to freedom.

The house was ill-treated during the Civil War. People stole shingles from the roof. Some

even broke chips off Thomas Jefferson's gravestone as souvenirs. A young woman who visited
Monticello in 1864 was upset to see that the
dome room Jefferson had carefully designed now
had "a thousand names scratched over its walls."

After the Civil War ended in 1865, the house
was abandoned. It was not forgotten, though.
Thousands of Americans traveled to the mountain each year to visit the third president's
home. But if nothing was done to repair the
house, soon there would be nothing left to see.

In 1879 Uriah Levy's nephew, Jefferson
Levy, decided to use Monticello as his summer
home. He set about restoring the house. It was a
big project, though, and one that he would not
live to complete.

Levy remodeled the house's interior. He
brought in expensive furniture. Jefferson Levy
placed a heavy, carved bed in Thomas Jefferson's bedroom. He hung thick draperies at its
head.

Jefferson Levy replaced Thomas Jefferson's alcove bed with a heavy, carved bed.

Tourists still came from all over the country to wander the grounds and tour the home of the third president. By the turn of the century, thanks to improved roads and trains and the invention of the automobile, fifty thousand people were coming yearly.

The Levys set up visiting hours to accommodate the visitors. Some of the eager tourists

Monticello in 1880. The job of restoring the mansion was too big for Jefferson Levy to complete in his lifetime.

ignored the rules, though, and the crowds were more than one family could control.

Maud Littleton, who was married to a New York congressman, was one of the visitors. She got the idea to turn Monticello into a public memorial and restore it to look as it did when Thomas Jefferson lived there.

Littleton formed the Monticello Memorial

Association, which worked for years trying to raise the $500,000 needed to buy the house. Several other groups joined in the effort to preserve Monticello. In 1923 they formed the Thomas Jefferson Memorial Foundation. They asked the American people to help their cause. Children from New York City even sent in penny donations. Finally, they had enough to put a partial payment down on the house.

Monticello became a public memorial on July 4, 1926, exactly one hundred fifty years after the signing of the Declaration of Independence. It would take fourteen more years before the foundation was able to raise enough money to begin restoration of the thirty-five-room mansion and its grounds.

The foundation hired carpenters to replace rotting beams. Workers cleared some of the trees to build new and better roads. That was the "easy" part.

Tracking down the original furnishings that

had been sold over a hundred years before was like detective work. The foundation members had to locate Thomas Jefferson's descendants, who had inherited some of his furnishings. Other artifacts were not tracked down for years, and often turned up in strange places. For example, Jefferson had given a wooden model of a Roman pitcher to the artist Thomas Sully in 1821. It turned up at a country auction in Pennsylvania in 1974. An alert shopper spotted it and returned it to Monticello.

The Garden Club of Virginia, which aided the foundation in restoring the gardens, found help from the perfect source—Thomas Jefferson's own "Garden Book." It contained carefully kept records of his gardening and landscaping plans, and listed each flower and vegetable he planted, and where. The Garden Club planted as many of Thomas's favorite vegetables as they could, including tennis-ball lettuce and Chile strawberries—and, of course, peas.

There is still a lot that twentieth-century people do not know about how Monticello looked and how people lived in Jefferson's time. For this reason, a team of archaeologists spends long hours looking for traces of Monticello's past that lie buried underground. After carefully digging up several thin layers of soil, they were excited to find a pattern of broken stones. Based on careful analysis, they identified these as the stone foundations of the small structures on Mulberry Row, where some of the slaves lived.

The detective work at Monticello will probably never end. Planning for the 250th anniversary of Thomas Jefferson's birth in 1993, Monticello's archaeologists and historians turned their attention to Shadwell, Jefferson's birthplace and childhood home. Although Shadwell no longer exists, the clues about the people who lived there, its houses and outbuildings are hidden in the ground.

Monticello was chosen as the site of special

exhibits and historical conferences in 1993.

Thanks to all of this hard work, Monticello has regained its original beauty. But the work hasn't ended. There is always more to learn about Thomas Jefferson, his home, and how Monticello's residents lived.

CHAPTER 5

VISITING JEFFERSON'S MOUNTAIN

For years, Thomas Jefferson and his family had to travel up steep, muddy roads to get to Monticello. When he took his friend Margaret Smith on a carriage ride she became alarmed at the rough mountain roads. Although Thomas was used to the jostles and bumps that rocked the carriage as it rode over fallen trees and large rocks, she wasn't. In fact, she directed the horse-drawn vehicle to stop so she could walk around the largest obstacles.

And Margaret wasn't the only one who felt this way. A lot of Thomas's visitors made comments about the "steep, savage hill" they had to ride up to get to Monticello.

They would have been surprised at the

paved roads leading up to Monticello today. Small buses transport people—500,000 every year—up the long driveway to Monticello's east entrance.

As visitors wait for a tour guide to lead them up the brick walk and through the columns of the portico, they have time to look at the famous house. Its design is symmetrical—the same on the right as on the left. Two dark green shuttered windows let in light on either side of the portico. Resting comfortably between two tall tulip poplars is the house. These trees were planted when Thomas Jefferson was alive—he may have planted them himself.

Visitors realize just how many interests Thomas Jefferson had as soon as they step into the entrance hall. This is where he greeted his guests, and it was also his museum room. Here he displayed maps, paintings, a buffalo head, the jaw of a mastodon, Native-American artifacts, natural-history specimens from the Lewis and

Clark expedition, and more. The entrance hall is not as crowded with objects as it was in Thomas Jefferson's day. They were all sold after his death and the search to recover these objects continues today.

There is a concave mirror hanging on the wall, and when people look in it, they see themselves upside down. The seven-day calendar clock that Thomas had specially made hangs over the entrance.The entrance hall is separated from the parlor by a pair of "trick" doors. The glass doors are connected by a chain under the floor. When one door is opened, the chain forces the other door to open with it automatically.

In the dining room, Thomas had revolving shelves installed. Kitchen workers standing outside the room placed food on the shelves. Then they turned the shelves around, and the family picked up the food inside. Thomas had probably seen this practical invention elsewhere, and adapted it to suit Monticello.

The library at Monticello.

From the entrance hall, visitors move through a small sitting room into Thomas Jefferson's library and study. One of Jefferson's granddaughters wrote that the library contained "more love of liberty, wisdom, and learning than any other private spot in America." The books in the library are the same titles and editions that Thomas sold to the United States government.

In the study, Jefferson's polygraph catches many people's eye. It was his way of "Xeroxing" papers instead of copying them by hand. He attached the polygraph to his pen, and it copied each letter as he wrote it. This saved a lot of time, since it is estimated that he wrote about 50,000 letters during his life.

Jefferson's telescope also sits in the study, pointing out toward the sky. Jefferson loved astronomy and learned to calculate eclipses. He was fascinated by the moon and planets. His alcove bed, where he died in 1826, fits snugly between his study and bedroom.

With its huge windows reaching to the floor, Monticello's parlor is a sunny place. Paintings and mirrors Thomas bought in France line the walls. A piano and Kirckman harpsichord dating back to Jefferson's day stand on the parquet floor. It's easy to imagine Martha Jefferson playing the piano while Thomas played his violin in the pleasant room.

Fire regulations do not permit visitors to view the dome room or Monticello's upstairs bedrooms. The narrow stairs Jefferson designed to save space would make it very difficult for a large group of people to escape these rooms quickly in an emergency. But people can visit the dependencies and tour the grounds.

The dependencies are beneath the terraces. The icehouse served as a refrigerator in Thomas Jefferson's day. Blocks of ice were carried in and used to chill food here. The smokehouse is where beef was smoked and dried to preserve it. In the kitchen, cast-iron pots hang in the fireplace, where meals were cooked over an open fire. Ceramic jugs, used for storing food or supplies, sit on the brick floor. A passageway under the house connects the dependencies. Visitors can follow the route from the north side of the house to the south. From there, a short path leads to Mulberry Row. Part of Mulberry Row has been excavated, including a stone house where the workmen who helped build Monticello lived. Signs and stone markers explain the rest of the archaeologists' findings.

Beyond Mulberry Row is Thomas's vegetable garden, situated on the sunny slope. In warm weather, tomatoes, peas, and other crops grow in orderly rows. Nearby, colorful flower beds circle the west lawn.

From the far end of that lawn, people get a different view of Monticello—they see a domed roof sitting over another columned porch. Turning around, they look out on the trees, valleys, and hillside farms. This was one of Thomas's favorite views.

At the foot of the mountain is the Thomas Jefferson Center for Historic Plants. Many people, especially gardeners, enjoy hiking to the center. The staff collects and raises plant varieties that were popular long ago but are uncommon now. They also present exhibits on early American gardening. Visitors can buy seeds of

Thomas's vegetable garden.

flowers and vegetables grown at Monticello for their own gardens. Also on sale are young tulip poplar trees. They are the "offspring" of the two big old tulip poplars planted in Jefferson's time!

If visitors want to, they can take a short hike to the family burial grounds, situated where Thomas's favorite oak tree once stood. Each year on April 13, Thomas's birthday, a wreath is placed on his grave. The marker that people see today replaced the original one, which was damaged by vandals in the years that Monticello became run-down. The small, wooded cemetery has been restored, too.

Every year, on July 4, the anniversary of the Declaration of Independence, Monticello is home to a special government ceremony. On that day, people born in other countries become citizens of the United States. This traditon would have pleased Thomas Jefferson.

The story of Thomas Jefferson's life and the story of Monticello are inseparable. Monticello is a brillant beacon that sheds light on the ideals of the country Thomas Jefferson helped to build.

Monticello: A Historical Time Line

1743   Thomas Jefferson is born in the English colony of Virginia.

1769   Construction of Monticello begins; Jefferson first serves in the Virginia House of Burgesses.

1772   Jefferson marries Martha Wayles Skelton.

1776   Jefferson writes the Declaration of Independence.

1781   The British surrender to George Washington at Yorktown, ending the Revolutionary War.

1782   Martha Jefferson dies.

1783   The United States and England sign an official treaty declaring the end of the American Revolution.

1784   Jefferson travels to France to set up trade agreements with European nations. There he observes European architecture and buys furnishings for Monticello.

1785   Jefferson becomes minister to France.

1789   Jefferson returns to the United States to become secretary of state and rebuild Monticello.

1796   Jefferson completes his plans for remodeling Monticello.

1797	Jefferson becomes vice president under President John Adams.
1801	Jefferson becomes the third president of the United States.
1809	The rebuilding is complete; Jefferson retires to Monticello.
1815	Jefferson sells his books to the United States government. They form the basis of the Library of Congress.
1826	Jefferson dies on July 4, fifty years after the signing of the Declaration of Independence.
1831	James Barclay buys Monticello. He tries to raise silkworms there, but fails.
1834	Lt. Uriah P. Levy buys Monticello.
1861-1865	The Civil War years; the Confederate government takes over Monticello.
1879	Jefferson Levy begins to restore Monticello.
1909	Maud Littleton visits Monticello; she forms the Monticello Memorial Association.
1923	The Thomas Jefferson Memorial Foundation is formed to purchase and restore Monticello.
1926	Monticello becomes a public memorial.

1938   The work of restoration begins.

1940   The Garden Club of Virginia starts to restore Monticello's gardens.

1954   Workers strengthen the mansion's structures.

1993   Special exhibits and educational conferences honor Jefferson's 250th birthday.

Visitor Information

Hours
8:00 A.M. to 5:00 P.M., March through October.
9:00 A.M. to 4:30 P.M., November through February.

Tours
House tours are offered continuously during hours of operation; tours of the grounds are conducted between mid-April and October, from late morning until early afternoon; the house and grounds are handicapped-accessible. Brochures are available for self-guided tours of Mulberry Row and the vegetable garden.

Special Events
Naturalization of new American citizens takes place on July 4 every year at Monticello; an annual wreath-laying ceremony is held at Thomas Jefferson's grave site on his birthday, April 13.

The Thomas Jefferson Visitors Center
Displays a permanent exhibit of more than 400 items owned and used by the residents of Monticello; the film *The Eye of Thomas Jefferson* is shown daily at 11:00 A.M. and 2:00 P.M.; the Visitors Center is located on Route 20 near Interstate 64, two miles west of Monticello; the Charlottesville and Albemarle County Convention and Visitors Bureau, in the same building, provides information on places of interest in the area.

The Thomas Jefferson Center for Historic Plants
Features exhibits and gardens that resemble as closely
as possible those grown in Jefferson's day; sells offspring
of Monticello plantings and other historic varieties;
located on the grounds of Monticello.

Additional information can be obtained from:

Development and Public Affairs Department
Monticello
P.O. Box 316
Charlottesville, VA 22902
(804) 295-8181

*Charlottesville and Albemarle County Convention and
Visitors Bureau*
P.O. Box 161
Charlottesville, VA 33902
(804) 977-1783

INDEX